*Praise for*
*How to Catch a Swamp Frog*

"Nostalgic, engaging and relevant... Dr. Clement shows us how life's simple memories can make us better at who we are and what we do."

Debbie D'Amore
Pima County Deputy School Superintendent

"Dr. Clement reminds us that teachers change the world one student at a time. It is his relationships with those teachers that burn in his memory; a fire lit by ordinary men and women who instinctively knew how to ignite the extraordinary in their students."

Arizona State Senator
David Bradley

**Legendary Teacher Stories**

# How to *Catch* a Swamp Frog

Author:
Nicholas I. Clement, Ed.D.
Ernest W. McFarland Citizen's Chair in Education
Northern Arizona University

Published by:
Teachers Change Brains Media
Tucson, Arizona 85737

*Marketing Consultant – Tim Derrig*
*Cover design & production - Pattie Copenhaver & Steven Linebaugh*
*Portrait photography – Robin Stancliff*

# Contents

# Dedication

To my legendary family, wife Jolene, daughters Kerstin and Christina, Son-in Law Tim and grandkids, Timmy and Kyle. You never let me give up trying to find my swamp frog and encouraged me to share my stories.

# *Acknowledgements*

This book has been bouncing around in my mind like a shiny steel ball in a pinball machine for 25 years. You might wonder why I am starting with a pinball metaphor. In the spirit of full disclosure, I got addicted to pinball my senior year at the University of Michigan. Although it never got to the point that I quit school to follow a pinball wizard dream, my long study breaks may have contributed to that extra semester of summer school. Hard as I tried to concentrate on studying for my psychopathology final, I couldn't resist walking down the street and up the dark narrow arcade staircase, chasing that distinctive free game clack. I think there is some irony in that story, but I am not going to refer to it as ironic because I wasn't paying attention in Mr. Pott's English class the day he taught irony, satire and simile.

In pinball, it is all about keeping the ball in play. You need good fortune to have the ball keep hitting lots of bumpers and good timing hitting the ball with the flippers. Authors also need good fortune and timing to keep their ideas alive until they hear that "I got it published" clack.

I was incredibly fortunate in my life to be taught and coached by many legendary teachers. My good fortune continued during my 35 year career as a school principal and superintendent. I was able to bounce off hundreds of legendary teachers "bumpers" and had the unique opportunity to observe and experience their classroom artistry every day.

I attribute the good timing of this book to a number of people and organizations who collectively kept those flippers active by encouraging me to write the stories down that I have been sharing and acting out in presentations for years. I want to acknowledge Northern Arizona University and specifically the College of Education Dean, Dr. Michael Sampson for providing me the time and flexibility in my position as the Ernest W. McFarland Citizen's Chair in Education to pursue and complete this book. I also want to recognize the Flowing Wells School Board, staff and community for the profound influence they had on my professional life which is reflective in every word written in this book. Thoughts to words, words to pages, pages to chapters and chapters to a finished book would not have happened without the encouragement of my brother Clark and the guidance from my advisor, Tim Derrig.

*Chapter One*

*Legendary teachers still insist*
*and believe they are mere mortal even*
*after we find them 20 years later*
*and express our deep gratitude for*
*changing our lives.*

# In Search of Legendary Teachers

July, 1992 and I am beginning my three hour flight back to my home town anxiously anticipating my 20th class reunion. My in-flight entertainment became a lively conversation with myself regarding all things reunion. How many classmates will show up? I recall there were 72 in my graduating class. Before you begin to think I am a memory genius, 72 in the class of 72. The older I get the more my brain loves those built in mnemonic devices.

Now that I brought up memory, next thought is that I should have had a memory strategy for finding my car when I got back in a week. Walking around for an hour looking for your car in the Tucson summer heat as you drag your suitcase up and down the rows is not a great way to end a vacation, although one time it did get me out of paying the weekly fee. The parking attendant was watching from her booth and felt my pain along with guilt for laughing as I began to melt. Now people tell me that you cannot lose your car because most have that button you push and the car will wink their headlights and honk your name. Not sure that technology was around in '92 and today it only works if you remember at least the parking structure level.

Second memory thought, as my ears make their final pop signifying cruising altitude: How would I deal with that awkward moment when I meet someone whose "Class of '72 Hi" badge is covered and my brain goes into name freeze? What if it was a girl I dated? Worse yet, what if it was a girl I never dated but wanted to and my memory decided to pay me back for the time that I finally found my car only to discover I left my keys in the security tray. That would be beyond awkward. The questions just kept coming and before I realized it, ears were popping again as the wheels touched down. Flying is supposed to be stressful, preparing for reunions is not, but I sure was giving it a good shot.

Our reunion was nothing fancy, a golf tournament followed by dinner held at the clubhouse. As I recall, about half the class attended. Our foursome kept score for about three holes, and then not only did we stop keeping score, a number of other foursomes merged with our group. This seemed to be happening all over the course and at the end of the tournament, no trophies were awarded because everyone was disqualified for inaccurate score cards and multiple violations of golf rules and etiquette.

We did much better with the dinner which went late into the night without any reunion rule violations. Not one "Look, I can still fit into my prom leisure suit" or "Late arrival in a car we knew you couldn't afford." The girls didn't wear jeans and the guys didn't grow extra facial hair to protest the dress code which was in effect during our high school years.

I was student council president my junior and senior year and ran on a change the dress code platform. I confess that I ran unopposed both years. So much more impressive if you leave certain details out of stories about your life. If my mother was alive, she would have made me recall this book and set the record straight, so I will save the expense.

After two years of meeting with our principal, superintendent, and school board, we were finally victorious with the board voting in March, 1972 to change the dress code allowing boys to grow facial hair and girls to wear jeans. Again,

I need to tone down the celebration and accolades with a small detail. The school board made these changes effective beginning in the following school year because they were afraid all the boys would show up for June graduation with a three month shadow.

I expressed my outrage and disappointment publically at the last school board meeting before graduation. I did not share that most of the guys in my class, except for Kevin, were just entering the peach fuzz phase. Graduation was never in jeopardy of a facial hair revolution. That detail would have definitely taken away from my two year stand against the establishment. I also needed to temper my protest because of a little incident involving me taking a week off during my senior year and going down to Florida to visit my brothers, who were working and going to school near Orlando. Five unexcused school days didn't put me in a real position of strength with the school board. If you are wondering, Kevin sported side burns for his senior picture that would have rivaled Peter Fonda from the movie *"Easy Rider."*

Although no one at the reunion seemed to remember my courageous fight for dress code freedom, we did have plenty of memories to talk about. My forgetting name fears were overrated as were the number of girls I thought I dated.

Back in my seat for the return flight and again, the conversation between Self-1 and Self-2 (apologies to Dr. Seuss) starts up even before the plane starts to taxi. First, I conduct my own personal flight check: keys in pocket – check, sitting in correct row and seat – check, note difference between reading light and flight attendant call button – check, and seat upright – check. I know flight attendants mean well, but you do get that look when you mistakenly hit the call button and I hate getting blamed for not having my seat up when it really was the passenger on the previous flight's fault.

Now that I completed what I call airline nesting behavior, I am ready to settle back and take a short nap, hoping that my parking location comes to me in a dream. Sleep was the furthest thing from what my brain wanted to do.

The wheels had just retracted and my mind was rapidly rewinding all the stories we told at the reunion, stories about our experiences as friends and classmates. I was awestruck with the amount of detail we could recall going back as far as kindergarten and even younger.

Details like having birthday parties at Vance's house. His parties were the coolest because some of us got to sleep over and his bedroom was in the basement at his house on a farm. His parties lasted all day. We recalled and told stories about how his dad would periodically come down and throw money on the basement floor and we would scrambled to get those pennies nickels and an occasional dime. Another memory we shared was how his dad would tie a saucer to his tractor and pull us in a circle on the snow until we couldn't stand straight. I was reminded that at one party, I was in the saucer and it hit a frozen cow pie at about 20 miles an hour and I became airborne landing in a snow drift. Another year, I fell in the ice walking across Vance's pond. What great times!

We laughed about our first class performance in kindergarten; all dressed in pajamas and singing "Up on the House Top" on the stage over the basement cafeteria. Stories triggered more stories. Stories about being in the fifth grade safety patrol where the older kids wanted nothing to do with your hands going down until traffic was clear. They ignored us even though we wore that impressive white webbed belt and sash with a badge. Someone remembered the ultimate safety patrol job was walking the morning kindergarten students home at lunch. You got to wear the coveted red captain badge, and more importantly, the kindergarteners followed your every move and direction. They stopped when you stopped and walked in a straight line like ducklings following mom to the pond.

We needed another full day just to talk about field trips. One we all remembered was fifth grade where we traveled to Kalamazoo to visit the Be-Mo potato chip factory. Ms. Scofield was our teacher, Mr. Skillman was our bus driver and we rode bus number five. We relived that day on the ninth and tenth hole with what now was a twelve some, talking about the Be-Mo sights, sounds, smells and tastes. You could actually feel the machinery vibrating and there is nothing that can compare to the memory of eating a fresh hot potato chip before it falls into the package. We worked on our math, counting the number of chips in 10 bags and then finding the average. I wonder when we changed from average to mean. The plane must be hitting a higher altitude because my mind is wandering more than usual. Someone recalled that we also got to taste cheese puffs right off the pile after they sprayed them with an orange mixture. The Be-Mo guide told us it was cheese; please don't mess with my memory by revealing the true ingredients.

The stories that really ruled the reunion were about our teachers. Everyone had a favorite teacher story or two or three. Stories about the shop teacher, Mr. Thompson who would stay after school every day for hours helping most of us create beautiful walnut-stained tie racks and perfectly shaped baseball bats. My shop projects weren't works of art by any means, but Mr. Thompson still worked tirelessly when I stayed after school fixing them. Father's Day gift time and my plan was to use the lathe and create a futuristic pencil holder shaped like two inverted trapezoids. I took the wood block and drilled six holes. Everything was working according to the plan, no after school work on this project. My dad would be so proud and he would definitely be putting this gift on his desk in his formal law office rather than hiding it in his closet like the ash tray I made him in eighth grade art. The art teacher carved a C+ on the bottom before it dried. She was strict about not changing our grades.

I locked my block into the lathe and proceeded to place my blade on the wood and with great precision, sculpted my masterpiece. There was only one minor problem. I should have waited to drill my holes until after my lathe work. On the positive side, Mr. Thompson's after school tutoring in wood putty application techniques has served me well in my future home repair projects. My dad proudly displayed my project on the front of his formal desk as though I had received an A+. I really got a C- but at least Mr. Thompson wrote your grade in pencil which eventually wore away.

Another teacher we had stories to share about was Mrs. King, one of our sixth grade teachers. Mrs. King would stand in the same spot every day at recess. When it was time to come in, she did not yell, blow a whistle, or ring a bell. Mrs. King would pull out her handkerchief and silently wave it about three times. We could be three miles away playing baseball or soccer, but we could clearly see that hanky come out and would race to get back to our class and into our seats. We did not run for fear of the consequences of being late, we ran for excitement because math relay would start when we were all in our seats. Mrs. King knew we loved math relay. Most important, Mrs. King knew how to motivate with kindness.

As I continued to relive the reunion and more stories kept coming, I started to have an "aha" moment. As teachers, we live for those times when our students' faces light up signaling "I got it." My moment intensified the more I thought about why we could remember such incredible detail about certain teachers and the experiences they provided. Then it hit me right about the time I was making sure my seat was upright. We didn't keep our golf score or get involved in the normal reunion "I made it big" bragging because we spent all our time searching for our legendary teachers. Our search was conducted with stories. Stories rich with details we remembered because of the relationships and positive influence these teachers had on our lives.

We know our brains have limited memory capacity, and whether we give it permission or not, our brains will erase memories and details it doesn't believe are relevant to our success. The obvious example is that when I get to an airport, I am too focused on where I am going and worried about doing my flight check that my hippocampus decides that the parking location takes up too much short term memory space. On the other hand, I can remember that Mrs. King waved her hanky three times and that Mr. Skillman took us on bus number five on a field trip we took 50 years ago.

I have taken my search for legendary teachers from a class reunion conversation to writing a book filled with legendary teacher stories. Why write a book about legendary teachers? The initial reason was personal and then broadens to a belief that these stories could benefit the teaching profession. As I reflect on my life, I was fortunate to have many legendary teachers who influenced my decision to become a teacher. Writing these stories became a way to preserve this history.

This book is also written to provide new teachers and students considering teaching as a career choice, real life models to emulate. Veteran teachers will find that these stories validate your efforts in making a difference in your students' future. Lastly, I hope these stories inspire others to write and share their own legendary teacher stories. Don't wait 40 years to write your own book and when you do, send the first copy to your legendary teacher.

*Chapter Two*

*Legendary teachers have frog eyes.*
*Frogs have great vision.*
*They can see colors.*
*They can see bugs at night.*
*Some frogs even have three lids,*
*closing one for camouflage*
*while still being able*
*to see everything around them.*

# *How to Catch a Swamp Frog*

Legendary teachers have frog eyes. Frogs have great vision. They can see colors. They can see bugs at night. Some frogs even have three lids, closing one for camouflage while still being able to see everything around them.

I grew up on Mill Lake near Gobles, a small town in southwest Michigan. Michigan people are lucky because we have a built in GPS. When we want to show you where we grew up, we quickly raise our hand, palm forward, and point to our home. If you were from the Upper Peninsula, it is a little more difficult, and no offense to Texas or California, make those states with your hand and you are apt to break a finger.

My mom, Betty, had her hands full raising six kids. As a middle child, according to the birth order experts, I was supposed to make her life easier. Unfortunately, when I was five, those books hadn't been published yet. I had not just some, but all the normal five year old flaws, keeping my zipper up, constantly losing my gloves, difficulty hitting the toilet, putting my tongue on the frozen pipes, and eating school paste. Salty, gooey goodness!

One time I got off the bus after school without my gloves, which was not unusual, except this time it was after the morning my mom had rigged what she thought was a "Nic-proof" system, safety pins attaching gloves to my coat and backup yarn threaded through the sleeves. Although it was a particularly cold day, my mom made me walk back to school to try and find my gloves. Yes, there was about two feet of snow and it was about two miles. My best friend Terry lived on the way to school so I decided to stop and warm my hands up. After some hot cocoa, Terry and I decided to explore his farm. I had my excuse ready because I knew my mom was going to ask what took so long. I could have left my gloves at Terry's house so I stopped to look before I went to school. We did more scaring the birds roosting in the barns and playing on the tractors then we did looking for gloves.

On our adventure, we went into a smaller barn that I had never been in before when the unimaginable happened. I stumbled into a secret closet and before Terry could yell "Stop," there it was – a Santa Claus suit, including a full white beard and coal black boots. Terry's grandfather was a professional clown and during the holiday season, he and his grandmother were Santa and Mrs. Claus for Gilmore's, the biggest department store in Kalamazoo. He was the only Santa whose lap I ever sat on. He was the only Santa I told about wanting a *Stingray* bike for Christmas. As you might imagine, Terry had been told never to tell anyone his grandfather's occupation, especially his friends who had five or six more years as Santa believers. I was devastated. Never found my gloves, but never lost my gloves ever again.

If keeping me out of the neighbors' off-limits barns wasn't enough of a full time job, my mom had to contend with an outlier. Although I was proficient and preferred writing and eating with my left hand, she was convinced that the world was built for righties and worked diligently to fix that problem. Teachers didn't argue with my mom. The barber, Mr. Wilsea, didn't argue with my mom when she sent me back on my Stingray to get my hair cut shorter. *The Beatles* were just becoming popular. As much as I wanted to grow out my hair,

I secretly didn't mind because it meant that I would get that hot lather and shave treatment around my ears again. No one argued with my mom because no one ever won an argument with my mom. Just ask my dad.

November, 1962 began my right handed era. How do I know that is when I officially changed hands? Every day after school, I would come home and throw every handwriting paper, arithmetic ditto sheet (loved the smell of a fresh ditto sheet), art project and scholastic reader in a box. When I came home for a visit after getting my first teaching job, my mom told me I needed to clean out my room including my chronologically ordered school paper box. I don't care if you are 10 or 30, if your mom tells you to clean your room, you clean your room. It was like that scene in *Christmas Vacation* when *Chevy* Chase is stuck in the attic and starts going through old movies. I was mesmerized having elementary school flashbacks with every paper I touched. I even found PTA notes with the safety pin still attached with bits of shirt cloth.

There it was, a drawing titled 'My School" with two square yellow buses labeled No 8 and No 5 in the left of my brown school building with a chimney and stick smoke coming out of the top, a stick figure teacher with a stick bell in her hand with musical notes drawn above the bell on the right, two stick figure kids walking on the sidewalk and a bright yellow sun drawn in the far left corner with my name Nickey underlined three times. It was dated October 10, 1962. The next month's artistic masterpiece had the turkey traced on my left hand and the sun and my name Nic with no underlines in the far right hand corner. Never again did the sun and the son's name rise on the left hand corner.

As I reflect, my mom's passion for raising her kids the right way translated into numerous legendary teaching lessons that have had a great deal of influence on my career in education. I would like to share one of those important lessons.

My room was on the third floor of the only house my parents owned. Mom and Dad had a goal of providing a room for all six kids. They reached their goal, although your room reflected their financial situation at the time you got your room. My oldest brother and sister had beautiful rooms with built in cabinets and heat. My room was a converted attic with thin paneled walls and a pressed wood floor. One day, I put a hole in it bouncing on the bed. I tried to cover it up but the following Saturday morning a small squirrel found the hole and my mom found the squirrel running around my room when she went to clean. Her screaming "Nicholas Irving Clement" was a little louder than usual that morning. I believe middle names were invented so parents could quickly let their children know they were in big trouble. I told you, outlier!

Squirrels in the floor, bees in the walls, having to avoid banging your head on the slanted ceiling when you woke up in the morning…I loved my room, except the time my parents decided to have an impromptu fire drill in the middle of one bitter winter night. They brought an aluminum chain link ladder they threw out my third story window and told me to get out and climb down. Excitement turned into terror. Seems that my parents had not correctly measured the height of my window and the ladder was short, one full story short. I am now hanging on at the end of the aluminum ladder, in my pajamas as the temperature continued to drop. Part of me wanted to cry, part wanted to jump, and part couldn't resist putting my tongue on that shiny frosty handle. I survived, and as my mother predicted, the adversity made me stronger. At least it gave me a lead in to the real lesson.

Every night during the summer I would go to sleep with the sound of frogs. At age six, my mother finally let me go frog catching alone in the shallow swampy end of the lake. She gave me a net, told me to put on my red boots, and then let me go down to the lake. Red boots probably mean nothing to you, but the cool six year old boys in the 60s in Michigan wore black boots with hundreds of metal buckles. School days were longer in Michigan because it took so long for kids to get their boots off. Teachers would line up your boots by gender, girls on one side of the hallway and boys on the other. Black, Black, Black, Black, Red (Nicky written in black permanent ink on the side) Black, Black and Black. The red boots with a little right handed rubber strap (not even one buckle) were a hand-me-down from my oldest sister. Don't worry, I am over it; I know my parents were probably trying to save money to buy a longer fire escape ladder.

As I ventured out into the lake, I waded up to the top of those stylish red boots and stood all day in the same spot (probably was more like an hour, but time to a six year old is like dog years) waiting for the frogs to come jump in my net. To my surprise, no frog! My older brother came by and after coming out in the water, without boots (seniority has many privileges) and hitting my arm ("raising your sons not to hit each other on the arm" books had also not been written), he told me to set up a frog trap by turning over one of the canoes on shore and waiting all day. He also said I needed to sit by the canoe the whole time or the frogs wouldn't show up which allowed him to periodically check on me and hit my arm again.

At the end of the day, we turned the canoe over, and there he or she was, I did not know how to check because we wouldn't have that talk until I was much older. My dream had come true. In the dark shadow, I saw the biggest, slimiest green leopard frog I had ever seen. I slowly and tentatively went to grab him and he quickly jumped away. I had to repeat the whole procedure and routine all over again, but this time, with my brother holding the canoe, I crawled under, grabbed him quick and his slimy wiggle startled me so that I let up and he swam away. I was probably holding him in my left hand. Another round of canoe turning and arm hitting resulted in success, I held on to him long enough to put him in a big bucket and marvel at his beady, attentive eyes. Don't worry, I practiced catch and release because I knew my mother couldn't handle finding both a squirrel and a frog running around my room.

I know you are thinking, how is he going to take this story and relate it to legendary teaching? Wait for it…teaching is like catching a swamp frog – you have to quickly grab students' attention at the beginning of lesson and then fight hard to keep their attention or they will mentally squirm their way out. Going off to explore another barn rather than how to calculate the mean of 10 different numbers.

Legendary teachers understand that students come to every lesson with their brains jumping in all different directions and they are masters at setting up the canoe trap to get those brains focused. They know how to quickly start lessons by presenting discrepant events, puzzling problems, and familiar analogies that motivate students to drop what they are doing and work on coming up with solutions. They also demonstrate patience, yet quickly act to create a new challenge when their students seem to be most comfortable.

Legendary teachers don't sit back with their red boots on and wait for their students to jump in a net. Mr. Davis, my ninth grade biology teacher, fit this legendary teacher definition. We knew when we entered his class, even before the bell rang, our notebooks organized with our daily notes, quizzes and tests were to be on our desks ready for him to walk the aisle and check our work. He treated every minute of class as sacred learning time. He was tough, consistent and fair and we responded with respect and hard work.

I looked forward to Mr. Davis's class because I knew we would be exploring, engaged and learning something new and exciting every day. One of my strongest memories is the biology dissection labs. I am sure the formaldehyde had some part in the memory trigger. I actually liked the smell. I also liked the smell of the ditto sheets when the teacher had just run them, and as you recall, I had a fondness for paste. By the end of this book, you will think my mom deserved sainthood.

We dissected worms, starfish, clams and yes, frogs. I know, a bit ironic, but I am still fascinated with how similar the frog's anatomy is to the human. After we completed our frog dissection, we had a pin test where everyone's frog cadaver had a pin locating a different part of the frog's anatomy and we walked around the class identifying each pin on our clip boards.

I remember Mr. Davis's infamous leaf notebook project that our older siblings would warn us about as being scary hard. They were right and I still have mine and it is on my shelf next to my dissertation. The real reason for the learning and memory retention is that Mr. Davis created relevant, hands-on activities which challenged us intellectually, while at the same time didn't shut us down by being over our heads. He is a legend because he brought the right balance of compassion, high expectations, no-nonsense, and content expertise to our classroom.

Every day third hour, he quickly grabbed our attention, captured our curiosity and inspired us to learn. Thanks to Mr. Davis, my eyes still get beady and attentive when I study biology.

Chapter Three

*"Legendary Driver's Education
teachers have the patience
and wisdom to know
when NOT to use
the passenger brake."*

# *Start Flipping Your Pennies*

Quick, name your seventh grade math teacher. If you can name this teacher within one minute of reading this, email me their name and I will enter you in a drawing for a prize. You probably think I should exempt current seventh graders from this contest. If you are in seventh grade and you are reading this book, good for you. You deserve a prize without being in a drawing.

Seventh grade is not usually one of our memorable grades and singling out the contest to math greatly reduces the memory recall. If we had a "remember your kindergarten teacher" contest, my inbox would probably crash the server. Mine was Miss Ringle. Although it was half-day, Terry and I would always arrive early because we could not wait to see her smile and hear her kind, gentle voice give us guidance and direction. Fridays were the best. Graham crackers and chocolate milk for snack instead of the normal white milk and saltines.

I not only remember my seventh grade math teacher's name, Mr. Serrell, but right now, I could find his class, my seat, the pencil sharpener, and recall the exact time class started and ended. Math was first hour and his class was only three doors down from Mrs. King's sixth grade class, but it was seventh grade, a whole new world with new rules. Changing classes, a notebook for every class, no more recess, P.E. where we changed clothes and a rumor that there were dances with girls. Mr. Serrell was right at the door and his smile and caring voice immediately helped alleviate my first day jitters.

I could also tell you where on the floor we sat in a small group flipping pennies and keeping track of the number of heads and tails during our first probability lesson. To this day, I am amazed that our prediction that we wrote on our paper of half heads and half tails didn't come true. Another memorable lesson was where we threw two dice and he assigned numbers two through twelve to horses he had cut out and lined up at one end of the chalk board. Any time a horse's number was thrown, the horse got to move one space toward the finish line. At the end of the lesson, we had to calculate which horse won the most races and then figure out why. We discovered that although horse seven won the most races, it wasn't luck at all.

Mr. Serrell went on to be my seventh grade and J.V. basketball coach, track and cross country coach, and my behind-the-wheel driver's education teacher. One of my proudest moments was receiving my varsity letter as a freshman in cross county from Mr. Serrell.

I wanted to play football in the worst way, but my mother didn't feel it was safe, and as you may recall, no one won an argument with my mom, not even the football coach in a very small school. One homecoming half-time, I was up for King, riding on the back of a 1972 white *Mustang* convertible in my ill-fitting suit and way too wide tie, so jealous of the football players riding ahead of me in full pads and that intimidating black grease paint smeared under both eyes.

To be honest, I never totally embraced cross-country as a fun sport. It is a good thing we practiced on paths that went through woods and tall cornfields because I often had to veer off the course to lose my lunch. That was the up side. The down side was that during meets at other schools, those cornfields could become confusing and getting lost didn't help my finish times and our team score.

I remember Mr. Serrell did his best to motivate me. He would often take us out in the sticks (a mile past the boonies) and follow us in a station wagon as we ran back to school. Shouting words of encouragement out the window to the bringing up the rear group like, "Come on you guys, it's starting to get dark" and "The football team is already done with practice and they are hanging out with their girlfriends." I made up the football quote, but if "hanging out" was around in the 70s, he would have used it.

No matter how average or below average a runner I was, Mr. Serrell never gave up on me. He always thought I could be a better runner, a better mathematician and a better driver than I thought. Where I grew up, everyone learned to drive some type of vehicle at about the age of ten. When it came time for behind-the-wheel training, Mr. Serrell rarely had to put his foot even near the extra brake. No orange cones or school parking lots for his students. Straight to a major highway in a stick shift on the column *Chevy Biscayne.*

Did I mention that everyone in the town learned to drive on tractors and beater farm trucks but me? My dad decided that I needed to learn how to drive the right way and the only driving I did before that first terror stricken day on M-40 was on an old *Simplicity* riding lawn mower that had a stick that doubled for steering and a clutch. If I timed it just right, I could pop a wheelie at its maximum speed of two miles an hour. It took all day to mow our yard and even longer when I got stuck going too close to the lake. All day hunting swamp frogs, all day mowing the yard, all afternoon looking for my gloves...
detecting a pattern?

My turn to drive after my two female classmates had just expertly navigated the *Chevy* around town smoothly shifting gears with the precision of a *NASCAR* driver. Mr. Serrell always had his driver's education students drive to some fun and interesting destination. He was into relevancy before relevancy was in. I am gripping the wheel tighter than a swamp frog and we hadn't even moved from the shoulder on M-40. It's a muggy June day, but that's not why I was sweating. Mr. Serrell said, "Let's drive to Paw Paw and watch them bow and arrow fish for carp by the dam." Without giving you every car jerking, gear grinding, panic expression (everyone in the car) detail, it will suffice to say Mr. Serrell finally got to use that extra brake pedal.

Although it was watching people fish, it was like arriving to *Disneyland* for everyone in my car. They couldn't wait to get out of that car and run down the river bank as fast as if they were trying to be first in line at *Space Mountain*. As Mr. Serrell walked with me, giving me some much needed encouragement and confidence building, we turned to discover the Biscayne following and quickly gaining on us, Mr. Serrell put his track skills to work, running alongside the car, jumping in, and slamming on the parking brake. If there ever was a time and excuse to use a voice louder than his teacher voice, this was it. After he got out of the car and had time to quit trembling, he calmly said, "Nic, you need to remember to put the car in gear and set the parking brake next time."

I wish I could report that my driving skills dramatically improved after that close encounter with my allowance being garnished for the rest of my life to pay for my first *Chevy*, but no such luck. I think it was the first time in driver's education history that the brake pedal on the teacher's side had to be replaced. Nevertheless, Mr. Serrell never gave up on me.

He always allowed us to drive ourselves home at the end of the session so we could show off to our family. After hours of practice, I was starting to get the driving rhythm and building confidence. Another hot day in August and the entire family including my aunt, uncle, older cousins and brothers, and parents, were out in the yard. I had a little too much confidence and in an attempt to show off, I took the drive a little fast, crashing into the new wooden fence with the sound vibrating along every board and I am sure all across the lake. With the school car wedged between the bottom of the fence and the drainage ditch, I just froze not taking my hands off the 10 and 2 position as if that would make the humiliation go away. My dad had just a little extra concern in his face, being that he was the school district's lawyer.

Math class, driver's education, basketball, cross country and track coach, Mr. Serrell was always taking risks and working hard to improve his students' educational experiences. Spring snow did not stop him from having track practice. He designed and built an indoor pole vault venue in the gym. When the new fiber glass pole vault poles came out, he had his driver's education students drive two hours to Lansing to be the first to pick one up. The fact that the pole didn't fit inside the car did not deter him from his mission to provide state-of-the-art equipment for this team. One drove and the rest of us held the pole on the roof. The same flexible fiber glass design that was going to help break school records, created a real challenge going 60 miles an hour on an expressway.

Although I have more Mr. Serrell stories to tell, you are thinking, make him a legendary teacher already. You have run out of patience with me and you are only reading about a few things that happened 40 plus years ago.

Mr. Serrell is high on my legendary list because he understood the power of creating and building relationships with his students. He knew that we enter each new learning situation like I entered his math class for the first time, anxious, unsure and not wanting to fail. He also knew that every student brought a different background to each lesson and he adjusted his teaching accordingly. Knowing your math facts or knowing how to clutch and shift, Mr. Serrell started at your level and pushed you forward.

He was the most patient teacher I have ever known. A patient teacher trusts that with enough encouragement, modeling, practice and non-judgmental feedback, every student can learn and master a new skill.

Mr. Serrell considered his students part of his family. My dad suffered a massive heart attack in 1968 and I remember vividly my aunt coming to school and picking me up to go to the hospital. My dad spent months in intensive care and it was a very difficult time. I was on Mr. Serrell's JV basketball team at the time and he and the team provided incredible support. Legendary teachers connect with students on many different levels and their impact influences students for a lifetime.

I still struggle running, but I stick with it because Mr. Serrell stuck with me. Every time I feel like skipping a workout or not trying something that I don't think I am good at, I look at that varsity letter displayed at the center of my office wall.

Some years ago, I wrote Mr. Serrell and shared a few of these stories and let him know what I was doing and how he had influenced my life and career. I received a letter back and at the end he wrote the following post script, "You can call me Gary." Sorry Mr. Serrell, I just can't.

If you are wondering, I did get my driver's license. Once again, detail guilt comes into play. I did not pass on my first attempt. The examiner had a little problem with me not yielding at a yield sign and making a left hand turn from way over in the right hand lane in busy downtown Paw Paw. His exact words were, "Come back after you have had some more time driving with your mom." Just the words every 16 year old wants to hear after their driving test. I don't think it's a coincidence that eventually I moved to Arizona where you get lifetime licenses without a road test. I didn't win Homecoming King, but I am over it.

*Chapter Four*

*Legendary Drama teachers
always show students how and why
the show must go on.*

# *You are Going to Need to Improvise*

"Hey Nic, you want to try out for the school play?" "I don't think so, I can't memorize lines and I would be way too nervous to get on stage." This was the first of about ten conversations I had with my English and Speech teacher, Mr. Potts, before he finally convinced me that I could memorize lines and stand on a stage without throwing up.

I know I seem to reference throwing up a lot in these stories. Our cafeteria food was not that bad. I really liked those mashed potatoes and that meat stuff they would put on top. I especially enjoyed the sound the potatoes made when it hit the green plastic tray. It was always a challenge to use our spoons to keep the gravy in the middle without breaking the levy. The lumps helped a lot. I feel sorry for students today who have to eat with plastic sporkes on Styrofoam plates. Not near the fun.

I also knew that if I complained about the lunches, my mom would start making them for me. I recall she did make my lunch one time when I was in second grade. I couldn't take it to school because it was too big to fit on the bus. She had to bring it up to the school and present it to me as I am in the lunch line with all my friends. As I took the shopping bag with enough food to feed the entire school along with my name written in billboard size printing, my mom proceeded to do what she referred to as a "Nic Check": shirttail in – check, shoes on right feet – check, hair cut short – check, and zipper up – check. Unlike my airplane check, my mom did not do this quietly. My classmates never said a word because many knew my mom from after school and Saturday visits and they didn't want to be next. Bottom line, we all enjoyed the twelve baloney sandwiches, giant bag of Be-Mo potato chips, a full celery stalk, a bag of carrots and two boxes of Nilla wafers. At the end of every day, my mom only wanted the best for her children.

Surprise – I made the cast of my first school play. Now that I look back, Mr. Potts only had enough students trying out to fill all the characters in this play, but at the time he never mentioned it, giving me the impression that my Robert Redford type talent beat out all the other guys trying out. After the couple weeks of practice, Mr. Potts held a cast meeting and told us that he was sorry for picking such a bad play and that it was too late to change, so we would need to improvise. I was having enough problems learning my lines to worry about quality so I asked what he meant. He said that we needed to start having more fun in rehearsals and not be afraid to change some lines. This piece of Mr. Potts' wisdom has always stuck with me and influenced my teaching and leadership. If you are not having fun, your audience certainly is not having any fun.

With all due respect to the playwright, Mr. Potts was right; this play was a real stinker. Without giving away too much of the plot (I know some time you will be attending this play on Broadway and I do not want to wreck your evening), it was about a boy running away from home to Alaska and on the way, he ends up stopping to visit his girlfriend, who attends an all-girl private school and lives in a campus dorm with a well-meaning but very strict dorm mother. Boys were strictly forbidden.

We proceeded to take Mr. Potts' direction and change up lines, staging, and plot lines with every rehearsal being different from the previous one. Since the school had not produced a play in a number of years, we were all novices. He taught us the basics: to project and articulate our voices, timing, staging, and make-up and did it while treating us as Broadway stars. As our confidence and dramatic skills developed, we proceeded to take Mr. Potts' direction and improvise. Changing lines and expressions until the play was transformed into a fun performance.

Opening night and my entire family is sitting in the front row of our gym with the play being staged on the same stage where we sang "Up on the Housetop." Lights were dimmed and the curtain opens. I could see my family in the front row folding chairs and particularly saw my Grandma Elma's beaming smile.

Everyone will tell you that they had the best grandma growing up, but mine was the best. One of the greatest years of my life was fourth grade when I got to walk to Grandma's house for lunch. My parents had arranged for each of the six kids to have their year with Grandma. Lunch was incredible. Always homemade and today, Grandma would have had her own Food Network show titled Elma's Leftover Magic. To this day, I have never found anyone who could duplicate her chicken biscuits and gravy or her personal warmth and caring.

I could always ride my bicycle to Grandma and Grandpa's house any time I wanted. My Grandpa was an extremely hard working man. When I knew him, he was a handyman along with sharpening saws, cutting down trees and would often take his grandsons along on jobs to be both helpers and learn his work ethic. He passed away when I was in junior high and Grandma lived over twenty more years. Night or day, you could always count on two things at Grandma's house: great food and a kind soul. I think she thought my mom was a little too hard on me, so I got a little more attention. She taught me how to sew hot pot holders, make Christmas candles using hot wax poured over ice in a milk carton and how to make peanut butter cookies with perfect fork marks. The secret was dipping the fork in milk! Grandma will always live on and has a very special place in my heart.

During my lunch year, Grandma would let me take her pop bottles back to the corner store and keep the deposit. I didn't exactly tell her this, but instead of starting a college fund, I would take the pennies and buy candy at the store for distribution at recess when I got back to school. I am sure it was against the rules, as was playing marbles for keepsies (still have my prize peerie, cat's eye and steely), but isn't fourth grade when you are supposed to start exerting your independence? It was also the year I learned some of those bad words which I only heard my parents use on rare occasions. My mom, when my full name wasn't enough, and my dad would substitute certain animal names. I am sure the seniors who didn't vote for me as Homecoming King forgot that I was the fourth grade Candy Man.

As the play proceeded, there was a part early on when I needed to get out of the girl's dorm room because they heard the house mother coming. The script called for me to run and jump out the window fabricated on stage and fake like I fell climbing down a fake trellis. When the chaperone was gone, I would come back on stage with a sprained ankle and a small tear in my pants. The planned improvised part was that I would wear some polka dot boxer underwear which would show through the tear when I walked on stage limping. We did not have a big costume budget. All the actors had to find clothing at home which fit their parts. It should not have been a big deal because this play was not *The Lion King*. My part called for black dress pants. The only pair I found at home seemed a little tight.

First unplanned improv of the night was when I crawled out the window, my pants slit right down the seam and Grandma and the rest of Gobles got a glimpse of a polka dot full moon. I made a quick wardrobe change and limped on stage with the script calling for the girls to get a bucket of warm water to soak my sprained ankle. Second planned (but not by me) improv of the night, the other cast members, with Mr. Potts' permission and encouragement, brought on water that was iced down for hours prior to the play and then at the last minute the ice was removed. We had never practiced with water and without hesitation, I proceeded to plunge my foot into the bucket. I immediately reacted by yelling out some improvised dialog with words I learned on the fourth grade playground minus the animal name substitutions. The memory of my poor Grandma's face still haunts me. Let it suffice to say that it took a year before I got chicken and biscuits again.

In spite of jeopardizing my graduation, the play was a big hit because that was just the start of planned and unplanned improvisations. Mr. Potts made my legendary list because he taught me that teachers have to be able to think, adapt, and teach on their feet, transforming their not as great as they thought plan into a great lesson.

Mr. Potts taught me that legendary teachers work hard at identifying unique factors in students and strive to help their students recognize and accept those factors. His perseverance in convincing me and other classmates that we could memorize lines and act on stage and then his expert coaching to make it a reality reminds me of what I learned from my dad about the Petoskey stone.

The Petoskey stone is the Michigan state stone. You can only find it on the Lake Michigan shores. When we would spend time at Lake Michigan during the summer, my dad would walk with me and teach me how to recognize a Petoskey stone. This stone when it is dry, looks like any other stone. Gray with no identifying marks or color setting it apart from other stones. My dad taught me if you carefully observe the dry Petoskey, there are some unique features that warrant closer examination. That closer examination was to either spit on the rock, put it all the way in your mouth or kick it into the water. Want to guess which method I used? When a Petoskey stone is wet, it transforms into a beautiful fossil with deep brown hexagon shaped patterns. Like snowflakes, no Petoskey stone is alike. If you do nothing to the stone, it will dry and revert back to the gray non-descript state. The only way to bring the uniqueness of the stone out permanently, is to patiently polish it by hand. If you put a Petoskey stone in a mechanical tumbler, it will disintegrate because it is such a soft stone.

Every student has a unique factor, which we often see as gray and nothing special. Without legendary teachers like Mr. Potts, we never reach our potential. We are all soft stones at some time in our lives and need the care only a legendary teacher can provide.

I am not sure Mr. Potts knew it at the time, but when he asked "Hey Nic, do you want to try out for the play?" he was really asking, "Hey Nic, do you want to be a teacher?" I am forever grateful that he kept asking until I said yes.

Chapter Five

*Legendary teachers
expect you to exceed
your own expectations.*

# *Here are the Truck Keys*

Another memory test: What was your first job? Technically, mine was picking blueberries at Fritz's Blueberry Farm about a mile from my house. It does not count because in order to be considered a job, you have to have worked there at least a week. I got fired before the end of the first week. Nobody told me that having a blueberry fight with my friend, Billy, who was on my crew, was a violation of the employment contract. It also was not in the contract that we would not get paid for our buckets if they had too many green stems. I could have hired my dad to represent me in an unlawful dismissal suit except for two reasons. 1) I really didn't like picking blueberries, and 2) My dad only represented clients that he firmly believed were innocent and were treated unfairly.

My first real job was at 15 working for Uncle Jim in the family lumber company, *J.L. Clement & Sons.* Before you become impressed with my resume, I got this job more with my name than my skill and talent.

I was a better blueberry picker than a lumber yard employee. I just could not get the hang of the business. For example, Uncle Jim had his own unique system for organizing lumber and other supplies. If someone came in and asked for an 8 foot 2x4, and I was running the store by myself, plan on about a 15 minute wait while I wandered around the yard. If and when I found the piece, and the customer wanted it cut to a different length, plan on another 15 minutes. If they wanted it cut straight, come back tomorrow. It got to the point that customers would drive in the yard, see me alone, and then drive down to the local coffee shop and have coffee with Jim until he came back. I still have my *J.L. Clement & Sons* orange work apron, 45 years old and it looks new. Uncle Jim was smart not to give me any sharp tools to carry around.

In spite of the fact that the lumber yard gene had skipped over me, Uncle Jim never fired me. He had far more reasons than Fritz's. There was the time I went to deliver lumber and hardware for an entire garage. Uncle Jim would always assume you knew the location of every resident within a 60 mile radius. He would give you a name and maybe the lake they lived on or the color of the house. For me, he made an accommodation and would take his J.L. Clement & Sons flat pencil from behind his ear and draw a map on the load of lumber. As you guessed, I would have to pull over on the way, get out and look at the map about three times before I got to the right address. It was really a challenge when Uncle Jim would draw the map across the 2x4s, which always shifted about the same number of times I shifted. Probably needed a few more hours in the *Chevy Biscayne* before I moved to the big flatbed truck with a stick on the floor and a high low differential. Uncle Jim was even at our house when my unfortunate accident with the fence occurred and he still gave me the keys.

I was confident that I had arrived at the new garage location. No one home, so I unloaded and after two hours, I left so proud to see that pile of neatly stacked lumber, drywall and other supplies in the front yard in those two story high rear view mirrors. On my way back to the yard, in between going directly from first to fourth gear and driving down a lot of dead ends like a rat running a maze (left my map somewhere between the plaster board and plywood), I started to have some doubt. When I returned to the yard and as I handed Uncle Jim the truck keys, I said, "That was a brown house, right?" Uncle Jim replied, "No, it was a white house." Throw back the keys please.

On one busy summer Saturday, I was working with the other yard employees, my two older brothers, and two older cousins. They were out delivering lumber to correct addresses and making sure custom made doors didn't fly out on M-40. Just like my gloves, I never found those doors. Often times I was the fifth wheel being too many years younger than the youngest older brother/cousin to be part of the group. Say that five times really fast. Uncle Jim also owned a small Christmas tree farm and during the summer our crew needed to trim the trees so they would have the right shape for Christmas. I spent one week on the crew, using clippers while they got to use a machete. To be fair based on my track record, I wouldn't have let me anywhere near a machete. I did feel part of the group and did feel that this was the start of being accepted until my breathing almost stopped on day four and the doctor informed my mom that I was allergic to Christmas trees. Not only was I out of the club, we had to start having those gaudy fake silver trees that kept falling apart when you tried to decorate.

On this Saturday, as I was busying myself with jobs I could complete, sweeping saw dust and signing as a witness to wills my dad was preparing, Uncle Jim called my name. Did I mention that my dad and uncle had the first law and lumber one stop? My dad's law office was located in the same turnaround drive. I am sure the statute of limitations is up regarding having a minor sign legal documents as a witness.

Uncle Jim had received a call from a wholesale lumber yard in Grand Rapids letting him know that they had a large inventory of 2x4s and that if he could have someone pick up a load, they would give him a great discount. Uncle Jim did not hesitate, he threw me the keys to that flatbed truck and said, "Nic, I need you to go to Grand Rapids and pick up as many 2x4s as they can load on this truck." I coughed and spit out some of my grape *Nehi* pop through my nose. Uncle Jim was a pioneer in performance pay; we got a pop break every morning and when I got a little older, he would ask if I had a date that night. One time I said yes and he gave me a five dollar bill. From that time forward, he must have thought I was the most popular guy in school because I had a date every Saturday night. That may explain my delusions of dating grandeur on the plane.

After cleaning up my apron, I reminded him that I had never driven to Grand Rapids nor had I picked up that big of a load. Before I could run around town and find someone who needed a will witnessed, I found myself driving that beast of a truck, climbing a steep hill in Allegan, double, triple and quadruple clutching on my way to Grand Rapids.

First miracle, I arrived at the right lumber warehouse before the sale expired. Second miracle, I was able to back the truck up to the loading dock without running over Junior and his cat. Junior ran the yard and every lumber warehouse in Michigan had cats. The cat kept the mice population down and Junior was there to keep my self-confidence down. After we got the lumber loaded, I asked Junior to help tie on the load. He stood on the loading dock stroking his cat and replied in a deep real lumber man voice, "I load, but I don't tie." Now I have two firsts, a drive to Grand Rapids and having to tie about 1000 2x4s onto a truck with no sides. I was wishing now that Mr. Serrell had included this as one of our relevant experiences rather than the trip we took to Lansing to pick up a new fiberglass pole vault pole. My fingers have yet to uncurl.

There, that ought to hold the load. I should have questioned my tie the load like I tie my shoe technique when I saw that smirk on Junior and his cat's face. I waved good bye and began my journey. Things seemed to be fine until I started up the ramp onto I-131. Loads bouncing a little as I am following Mr. Serrell's instruction, give it some gas and look in driver's side mirror. What he didn't tell me was what to do if when you look, you see your entire load swaying then slipping off and merging onto the expressway before your truck.

I would have put out my orange safety triangles from my safety kit if we followed *OSHA* rules. I would also have a CDL endorsement on my driver's license to show the Michigan State Police if I wasn't 17 and too young to qualify to take the test that I would never pass.

Third miracle, I reloaded the load and retied it using a double shoe knot and made it, grinding and bouncing all the way back to Gobles. I will always remember jumping out of the truck and tossing Uncle Jim the keys, and although he didn't say anything, I could tell in his smile and the sparkle in his eyes that he had never been prouder of me.

My Uncle Jim and my dad, William, are two of my legendary teachers because they set high expectations, helped you develop the skills to achieve those expectations and were always there to recognize your achievements. Once you reached a goal, they let you bask in the limelight for about a day until the call came to pick up a bigger load in Kalamazoo and sent you off this time without a map.

They understood work ethic and the value of an employee deferred payment plan. We may have only received a pop and $5 for a date, but you cannot put a price tag on the college education we all received as our retirement annuity with the *J.L. Clement & Sons* Lumber Company. When you do the math, I continue to be the highest paid lumber delivery man in the world.

Legendary teachers like my dad and Uncle Jim believed you can achieve way beyond your own expectations. They kept throwing you the keys even when you didn't want to catch them.

*Chapter Six*

*Legendary teachers
treat every lesson as though they
are playing basketball for a
state championship or
playing the piano
on stage at Carnegie Hall.*

# You Didn't Practice This Week

Wednesday morning, 5:30 a.m. I am fully dressed laying in my bed in my third floor penthouse listening to the squirrels scamper around inside my walls, hoping that my dad will sleep in and forget about my piano lesson. I went through this same routine for years and he never forgot. "Nic, come on down and get ready to go out to Miss Filley's." Miss Filley was our piano teacher and she lived out in the country about halfway between Gobles and Allegan. I will skip giving you the mitten, your brain's hippocampus is a quick learner and would be offended.

Miss Filley was a stickler for procedures. My dad would sit in the parlor (computer room for all of you under 50) and I would take my red Modern Course for the Piano book, sit at the piano in the living room, and Miss Filley would say, "Play your scales, chords, and then your first piece from the book."

After my warm-ups and my song, which had titles like "The Tiresome Woodpecker," Miss Filley always had the same response: "Nic, you didn't practice this week did you?" and I would bow my head as if prayer was going to help and replied, "No." I never made excuses because that would always make things worse. Miss Filley wasn't a yeller, yet my head would always sink deeper when her glasses would slip down her nose and she would get a little closer and say, "You are never going to get better if you don't practice, so let's try the woodpecker song again." I would play it again without any noticeable improvement and then she would take out her little star box and affix a red star on the page right next to the title. She was tough, but fair. I cannot recall earning many gold stars. Red stars signified that your dad did not sleep in.

One of the biggest regrets in my life is that I did not take Miss Filley's advice and practice harder to earn some gold stars. If she had told me learning the piano would have made me the center of attention at parties and that it would help me when I had to cover music classes when I was principal, I would have listened. My music class coverage always turned into a disaster and I hide in the corner at parties.

Not practicing and learning piano is right there in my top five life regrets alongside being unsuccessful in water skiing off the lake ramp. On our lake, there were unwritten rites of passage and many of them were connected to water skiing. There were certain age benchmarks for mastering slalom, trick, barefoot, and ramp jumping. When it was your time to learn, tradition was that dad would always go out on the dock with his 8 mm movie camera and document your ramp jumping for the family film archives. He has some great footage of me leaning forward and hitting the water face first, me leaning back and hitting my butt on the ramp, and the best one – my right ski coming off in mid-air. Too bad *"America's Funniest Home Videos"* was not around at the time. Like the red boots, homecoming king, and my driving exam, I have moved on and it doesn't bother me.

Playing piano with the music was difficult enough. Recitals and competitions were brutal because you had to memorize your piece. I remember one holiday recital where Miss Filley's students would play a piece with everyone's families crowded into the parlor, listening, smiling and applauding after each student finished their song with a hand in front and hand in back bow. My poor parents. They must have thought I was getting back at them for the aluminum ladder incident. I froze right in the middle of "O Christmas Tree." I tried starting over as if the piano elves were going to show up that night and bail me out. No bow for me, I just slid off that piano bench as fast as I could hoping I wouldn't have to walk home that night. More than two miles and Terry was not home because he was helping his grandparents at Gilmore's hand out candy canes.

I cannot honestly say that Miss Filley taught me how to play piano, although I can still play a mean first stanza of "Fur Elise" with my right hand. She did teach me a priceless Legendary Teacher lesson: practice, practice, practice.

Legendary teachers practice their lessons every day and constantly change and adapt in an effort to achieve better student results. Their classrooms and lessons promote student engagement with more practice as the students begin learning a new skill. They understand the benefit of trial and error in the learning process by creating safe, nurturing classrooms which encourage experimentation, trial and error and guessing. Legendary teachers motivate and inspire students to take their practicing outside the classroom. Legendary Teachers don't stop the boat or the camera until their students land successfully.

One early morning activity my dad didn't have to call my name for was eighth grade basketball. I did discover some years after my dad passed away, the "never missed a piano lesson" secret. I always wondered how my dad could have the patience to wait in the parlor, listening to me hit those wrong notes and without a smart phone to text, tweet or update his *Facebook* page. My mom told me that Miss Filley's sister would cook dad a full farm breakfast and serve it in the kitchen while I was pounding my way through "A Chord Frolic." He always made sure to wipe any evidence off his face when I was done.

Like many small schools in the 60s, all our basketball teams had to share one gym. Based on seniority, eighth graders practiced at 5:30 a.m. I never missed practice. Basketball was my life. We had a basketball court in the donkey barn hayloft. We had five donkeys named Jack, Jenny, Burrs, TuesNic and SunDee. Jack and Jenny were the dad and mom, Burrs was born in a burr patch and the last two were named after the day of the week they were born and the kid who discovered the foal. My parents were pioneers in memory frameworks. As I look back, I am not sure why we had donkeys. We did ride them in the local Memorial Day parade, but having us on their back was not their favorite pastime and I still have the bruises to prove it. It might have been part of my parents' master plan to teach their kids responsibility. That did not go as planned, evidenced by the time my brother and I had to take our entire college spring break to clean their stalls because Jack was hitting his head on the ceiling. If we had thought of it, we should have contacted *Guinness Book of World Records* to get in the book for the world's record manure compost pile.

Playing basketball in the barn was a little tricky because there were no lights and the ceiling had exposed nails. You had to adjust your shot to keep from falling out of the hayloft door and keep from having to buy a new ball. That did not deter us from having some great games and during the winter you could get more aggressive on defense because the snow would break your opponent's fall.

I almost got to sleep in during my eighth grade year. Our basketball coach quit right before the season started. Principal Wade was new to the school and he was not going to let the team down. He took over the team and I was up before the rooster could crow every day.

It was my rooster; part of that caring for an animal master plan. My brother had homing pigeons, which I thought were very cool because you could put messages on their feet and take them away for miles and let them go and they would bring the message home. I am not sure my dad had the same passion for homing pigeons, especially when my brother left for college. My dad found a breeder who said he would keep them in the dark for three months so they would lose their homing instinct and my dad could get his house (pigeons would roost all along the housetop and drop presents) and life back. Three months to the day and all the pigeons started coming back. To make sure my dad didn't box them up again, they decided to teach him a lesson by bringing friends of different breeds with them.

One of the many mysteries of my childhood: One day, my rooster, who would not only crow in the morning but liked to crow at other times of the day and night, was gone. How is it that the pigeons that could fly were always at the house, but my rooster, which was not much of a flyer, just disappeared? Still not sure if that is ironic.

There were great advantages to having your principal as your basketball coach. Winter mornings in Michigan were chilly enough. Wearing those short practice shorts and tank tops really brought the temperature down. Having the principal who always had the keys and knew how to turn on the heat in the gym and hot water heater for the showers was a definite plus. During the day, we would also have team meetings in his conference room. I am sure the teachers were pleased when the principal would call us out of class for an hour team meeting. Here we were, 12 short eighth graders sitting around that big walnut table with the high back chairs talking about our upcoming scrimmage in Holland. It doesn't get more memorable than that.

Although my mom was totally supportive of me playing basketball, her sixth sense told her that I probably was not going to pay my way through college with my talents. She let me play left handed. In eighth grade, it was a real benefit to be left handed. Most players must have had their moms tell them that it was a right handed world too. I would be guarded as if I was going right and I went left. Mom never missed a home game although there were some games I wished she had. One game, I am at the line for a free throw. In the late 60s, the crowd would be respectful and quiet during free throws. Just as I did my pre-shot dribble, my mom yells out, "Miss that and you are on carrot juice for a week."

An away game I wished my mom had attended was another small school in our league, Saugatuck. I was making all my free throws and having the game of my life. I had scored thirteen points in the first half. A record for me, and if they had kept records for eighth grade basketball, I am sure it would have been a school record.

It was the middle of the third quarter and Coach Wade takes me out of the game. I couldn't believe it, a record in the making and I am on the bench. I finally asked Coach at a time out why he took me out of the game and he said, "You are not passing the ball," then he paused and his eyes got more telling, "and we are not winning the game." At the time, I immediately put his decision in my "life is unfair" gym bag. Now that I look back, this was one of his many brilliant legendary teacher moves.

The first lesson Coach Wade taught me was that Legendary Teachers step up and step in when extra-curricular programs are in jeopardy of being canceled. One could argue that in the big picture, eighth grade basketball is not significant and that we would not have been adversely affected if Principal Wade had decided he was too busy to pick up the whistle. I disproved this argument with the fact that it has been five decades and those early morning practice and game day details are vivid, alive and continue to influence and shape my life. Mr. Pott's would be proud. I am still using my debate skills.

The second lesson was that Legendary Teachers pass the ball. Teaching is not a one-on-one sport and legendary teachers talk with colleagues, plan with colleagues, and collaborate with colleagues every day. It is the only way we win the game.

*Chapter Seven*

*Legendary teachers always*
*have their GPS tuned to*
*an achievement goal*
*for their students.*

# *Don't Favortize*

Remember the movie *"City Slickers?"* If you are wondering how I am going to get from *"City Slickers"* to a Legendary Teacher lesson, like Mr. Serrell, be patient, keep your foot close to the instructor's brake pedal and trust that given time and practice, eventually I will make the connection. It might be a good idea to buckle your seatbelt and put your seatback up just to be safe.

A brief review for those of you who haven't seen the movie since it came out in 1991, and I know some of you weren't born yet. Billy Crystal plays Mitch Robbins who joins his two friends as they go on a vacation to a working ranch, going from city slicker novices to expert cattle drivers in 113 minutes. The magic of movies. Obviously, becoming a legendary teacher takes a lifetime of learning content, pedagogy, brain science and human psychology. Ease off the brake, I am already starting to connect the dots. There was one line in this movie that was like one of those song melodies you just cannot get out of your head. I could come up with some song examples, but just naming the tune could trigger a downloading frenzy on *iTunes*. My mind was so persistent that I wrote the *City Slicker* movie line down when I got home and filed it in my might need this for a book someday file. Years later, when I began work on this Legendary Teacher concept, I figured out why my brain wouldn't let me forget the line.

Near the end of the movie, the guys are feeling good even though they are totally on their own. Curly, the trail boss died and the other less than helpful trail hands abandoned the group. The three remaining characters, Mitch, Phil and Ed are yelling "yip yip yee haw" and the cattle are moving together in a tight herd making those sounds we have learned to recognize in a successful movie cattle drive: moo, moo, and moo. The boys are dressed for success in their chaps and hats. Then some adversity – rain and a lightning strike bringing down a big tree limb right in front of the cattle. At that moment, Phil yells at Mitch, "Where are we?" Mitch replies that he doesn't know. Phil in a panic yells back, "You mean we're lost, but we're making great time?"

We have all had teachers who made great time. I had a math teacher whose idea of bell work was to take long pieces of chalk in both hands and frantically solve problems, showing all his work on the green slate and creating a cloud of yellow dust so thick I don't think he could see us as we arrived to class. If you were too young to see *"City Slickers," Google* "classrooms in the '60s" for a *YouTube* clip which will explain chalk and green boards. Mentally, this teacher really didn't see us either. As students, our only active engagement was to yell "ding" when he reached the end of the board (Google typewriter). There was one prize job, the chosen few got to go outside and clean the erasers by pounding them on the outside of the school brick wall. This could sometimes take the entire classroom period and of course, during the winter it took time to get our gloves and boots on. Unfortunately, no one told us that chalk on bricks is like permanent marker on red rubber boots. I am sure the marks are still there, a memorial to less than effective teaching.

His passion to make great time in math and do all those equations quickly and accurately did not compensate for the fact that most of the time we were lost. He rarely took his foot off the math express throttle to slow down and would only occasionally ask, "Any Questions?" This was more to catch his breath because he followed it with about ten seconds of wait time before he was off amazing himself with how fast he could multiply two binomials.

Of course we had questions. You could see it in our puzzled eyes and the way our heads tilted to read his board work. You could see it in our poor test and quiz scores. You could see our minds wander away from math and into other classes like P.E. – can't wait for dodge ball, biology – is that formaldehyde I smell, or lunch – craving some mashed potato surprise. Of course we were not going to raise our hands and ask a question. A raised hand in this class would bring an immediate teacher sigh, the signature eye roll followed by that "your slowing me down, I must finish covering this chapter today" scowl. Nobody wanted that stress so we took the path of least resistance, sat there, nodded our heads, smiled and were thankful there were only 105 days left of the school year. We knew this because it was the one math fact our teacher made sure we knew. He reserved a small corner of the green chalk board in which he kept the countdown. He never missed changing this number and even wrote a note and underlined it three times in red chalk to our custodian, "Do not erase." Red chalk really left a mark. In my lifetime, I have never been to a doctor, dentist, veterinarian, lawyer, or a lumber yard who had a small chalk board in their lobby counting down the number of days to when they could finally quit serving patients, clients or customers. Cats and putty filled pencil holders – yes, a countdown attitude – never.

Legendary teachers make great time and they know exactly where their students are academically and where they want them to go. They take their content expertise and change, adapt, and transform it in a way that students can develop deep conceptual understanding. Stories, visuals, analogies, imbedded and natural data sets, inquiry problems, period costumes, role playing, labs, memory frameworks, field trips, innovative technology, whatever it takes to teach that specific concept at that specific moment to that specific learner. Legendary teachers never stop asking students questions, because their goal is to have students never stop asking questions. They call students by name, not by their hands in the air. Legendary teachers live everyday by the motto: Teaching doesn't happen unless learning occurs.

Legendary teachers have through experience and continuing their education developed keen intuition and can read and understand their students' facial expressions, body language and voice inflections. They act on this intuition by making subtle adjustments to the teaching throttle. They make chalk dust when they need to yet know when to lay down the yellow or red stuff when it is time to listen, question and probe. They also know when external factors like family issues are impacting learning and understand unless students feel emotionally and physically safe, learning is difficult. Legendary teachers are the ultimate crystal ball gazers without having a crystal ball. They know what is going to happen in their class before it even happens. It would have been great to have a crystal ball in fourth grade. I would have dominated the marble competition with the largest peerie ever.

Here's the analogy my math teacher needed written in the space replacing the days left of school countdown. Imagine your students' brains are like a big Velcro ball. Now think about all those ideas, concepts, problems, and questions teachers are throwing at those brains as smaller balls. Teachers need to know how to take those small balls and before they throw them, make all the little hooks needed to stick. Without the hooks, it is like throwing *Jell-O* against the wall. Underline it four times and no need for the custodian note. After reading it, they would have added another underline. Teachers who are experts at making those *Velcro fastener* hooks become legends. Students are quick to tell you which teachers are great hook makers, if we take time to ask and listen.

As superintendent, I took this advice: slow down and listen to your students. Once a month for the last nine years, I held student focus groups with twenty students representing grades four through twelve. These students represented eight different schools and were members of the district Student Congress. Student Congress met for an hour with the superintendent at different school sites. These meetings provided me an opportunity to stop my hectic pace and take time to ask students questions about a wide range of important topics related to how well the school district was achieving our mission, preparing students to be successful in the life after graduation. We developed a strong trust and I valued and respected their opinion. Sometimes, they brought up issues which required quick attention, while other times, their feedback was invaluable for our long range planning and continuous improvement.

During the last three years, I posed the following question at one of the Student Congress meetings: "What is a perfect teacher and classroom?" In an effort to encourage their honest and unfiltered feedback, I split the students into four groups of five, with an equal representation of grade levels in each group. Although I did not leave the room, I did not sit in on the discussion or hover. The students listed their responses on note pads and turned them in at the end of the hour.

The major theme emerging from the Student Congress group responses to the perfect classroom prompt is that they want their classroom to be more like their home. Students are greatly impacted by classroom appearance. Descriptors like clean and fresh, neat, colorful, encouraging posters and pictures of students on walls dominated their lists. They also listed these home-like attributes: up-to-date technology, soft chairs, and desks organized so students can learn from each other. Every focus group listed a class pet in their perfect classroom world.

Students were very passionate and articulate in describing their idea of the perfect teacher. Understanding, cares about academic achievements, sense of humor, and creative were consistent qualities found on the lists. The fairness trait was especially strong and was reflected in the following  responses: not too much homework-not too little homework, not the same tone, not mean, have fun when teaching a lesson, take control when needed, strict but not too strict, prepared, listens to student ideas, inspiring, hands-on projects, and doesn't roll their eyes at students. One group captured a strong theme in all the data collected over the three years when they stated "a perfect teacher doesn't favortize students." (Spell check doesn't like it, but I love it!)

Students want their classrooms to be like their home, including a pet and their teacher to treat them like family. Perfect teachers transform into legendary teachers after about twenty years.

Sometimes the brain will remember facts about weird and strange animals longer than more common animals. One of my favorites, the naked mole rat – the only cold blooded mammal, lives underground like an insect and has sophisticated vocal communication. A full grown adult can fit in the palm of your hand and looks like a saber tooth sausage, and he or she is not naked (fine little hairs all over), and is not related to the mole or rat family. I'll let you guess this one: I lay eggs, but I am not a bird. I have a tail like a beaver and a mouth like a duck. I have a venomous fang in my back leg that has enough poison to kill a dog. Congratulations, it is the duck billed platypus.

This legendary teacher story was one of those strange animals. Cattle drives, *Velcro fasteners*, chalk dust, *Jell-O*, eyes rolling in back of the head, giant marbles and typewriters leading to the simple yet powerful fact we should never forget: Legendary teachers know where they're going and make great time. They consistently ask students questions, listen intently to their answers and don't favortize.

*Chapter Eight*

## Grandma Newcomb's Legendary Fried Cake Recipe

2 c. white sugar
3T. shortening
½ c. milk
1 c. mashed potatoes
2 eggs
½ tsp soda
2 tsp baking powder
Nutmeg, salt, vanilla & lemon.
Flour to roll soft.

Cut into donuts.
Deep fry at 365 degrees

# Kids in My Class Don't Get the Red Spot

Interview day and I am not sure who is more nervous, me, as the new principal getting ready to lead his first interview team, or Ken Fitzpatrick, the new interviewee for an English teaching position. The table is set, representatives from the English department on both sides. Mr. Fitzpatrick enters the room and is directed to take a seat at one end, and I take my seat at the head table spot. The same spot where my grandpa sat every Sunday for dinner.

All ten of my family members had unofficial official assigned seats for Sunday dinner at grandma's house. Most seats were based on seniority. Mine was next to my mother on her right, so she could make sure I did not eat with my left hand. If it started to move towards a fork, she gently immobilized it. Who knew that my mom knew about neuroplasticity? We never missed a Sunday. Food was all homemade including Grandma's bread and rolls. Grandma always had two different pies for dessert and kept us guessing until she retrieved them from the back room where they were resting in a pantry next to the homemade strawberry jam. More than a few times, I knew we were having cherry and blueberry pie because the back room is what we would today refer to as a "time out" room. As a special dessert, sometimes Grandma would make her bare crust. She would take left over pie crust, spread it out in a pan without filling and bake it with cinnamon, sugar and butter until it was golden brown. One time in a restaurant when I was young, I tried to order bare crust at the end of the meal. I couldn't figure out why I got such a strange look from the wait staff.

Nothing was more comforting than walking in Grandma's house Saturday morning when she was baking her bread and pies. First her smile and then the aroma – what a combination! Monday wasn't so bad either. She would take her leftover Sunday dinner mashed potatoes and make fried cakes. Only Grandma could use her special touch to turn mashed potatoes into a yummy treat which begged to be dunked in milk. On the other end of the epicurean spectrum, a late night snack at my home might be saltine crackers in milk. I put a lot of miles on my *Schwinn Spitfire* bike riding to Grandmas at meal time.

Ken's interview started smoothly, and we had him introduce himself, give his background, and talk about how he found out about the position. I admit I was being a little more formal than other interviews, using the time to exert my principal authority. I had a month to do the classic new principal power moves, rearrange the office and buy some new furniture, order new business cards and name plate, and check to make sure my master key opened all the rooms. My experience is that fine arts departments are always a little possessive and they also have an in with the locksmith. This interview was my first time to really show my leadership stuff to faculty and I was going to take full advantage.

The first part of the interview included Ken teaching a brief lesson with the committee pretending to be ninth grade English students. The school had been following this interview process for all candidates for a number of years. Normally, the interview committees had enough content specialists to allow candidates to teach an isolated concept in ten minutes. Except for the time that we had a last minute science opening and the assistant principal and I were the only ones available for the interview. One candidate attempted to teach us the effect of nicotine on brine shrimp. She brought all the materials for the lab including live brine shrimp. It took us the entire ten minutes to take our net and capture the little critters. If the candidate had known about my previous frog catching adventure, they would have requested an all-day interview.

Ken's lesson went great. I do admit that I laid back and let the teachers answer the grammar questions. We often asked Mrs. King why we needed to learn grammar and spend so much time diagramming sentences. She was very wise not to have Diagramming Sentence relay after recess. Many of us would still be out playing soccer. Like piano, I wished I had spent more time focused on those past participles.

After Ken's lesson, I began to feel more confident, and when it came time for that last question, I was forceful and principal like when I sat up straight (another reason I sat next to Mom) looked Mr. Fitzpatrick in the eye and stated, "As you know, we have interviewed a number of candidates for this position, so Mr. Fitzpatrick, take the last couple of minutes of this interview and convince the committee that we should choose you over all the other finalists." Don't ask me to diagram that sentence.

At this point, candidates often begin to visibly perspire and some develop what I refer to as the map of the United States rash. It starts with Michigan (of course) at the neckline and then moves up until you can see Indiana and Ohio wrapped around their neck. Like a sweaty palm, it is a great sign because it signifies an increased heart rate and tells the interviewers you have heart. No sweat, rash or hesitation for Ken. He looked me straight in the eye and said, "The reason you should hire me is that kids in my class don't get the red spot. Thank you for the interview."

At this moment, the entire committee turned and looked at me with piercing eyes. Although their lips weren't moving, I could hear their conversation. "Ok, Mr. Know It All. You have been acting like a typical first year principal smarty pants. We needed new student desks before you needed new office furniture. What are you going to do now?" I know Ken didn't intend to do this, but he turned the tables, beads of sweat and the map of the Upper Peninsula were gathering on my forehead. I had no clue what he was referring to with his red spot summary and for a moment, started to have a flashback. There I was, staring at a pie tin of bare crust, sent to the pantry for excessive use of my left hand.

I tried to recover by sitting up even straighter and lowering my voice with my follow up question. "Mr. Fitzpatrick, could you explain to the committee what you mean by your statement that kids in your class don't get the red spot?" Ken did not utter a word. He paused in silence until you could hear all our hearts beating. Mr. Fitzpatrick took his glasses off, carefully laid them on the new office chair armrest, brought his chair closer to the table, and then slowly thumped his forehead to the table making a sound loud enough to startle most of the committee. He stayed like that for a few moments and then sat up, took his right forefinger and drew a circle around the part of his forehead which was red from pressing against the table and declared, "See this, not in my class." Brilliant answer! After one of the shortest interview selection meetings ever, Ken was hired.

Your dream as a principal is to have a newly hired teacher's first week in the classroom performance match their interview. When it doesn't, you suffer, the interview committee suffers, and most distressing, the students suffer. I jumped on my old office chair (got the message, returned the furniture) and did my principal happy dance with a couple fist pumps after my first classroom visit and formal observation of Mr. Fitzpatrick.

Any given day, any given hour, if you walked in Ken Fitzpatrick's English class, you would observe his students on task, actively participating in relevant activities. Group work, class discussions, seat work, and his lectures were relevant, interesting and student centered. Even the signal he used to make transitions prevented the red spot. When he wanted students to focus, he would call out, "I saw Elvis." His students would quickly respond with "uh huh" in perfect unison and perfect Elvis baritone pitch. On some days, Ken would add a twist and shout, "Where?" and one student would get to call out a location in Tucson, like *Subway* on River Road." His seamless, smooth transitions minimized distractions and maximized learning time.

Mr. Fitzpatrick eventually moved to another school in another state. A year later, he stopped in my office to say hello. I asked him what brought him back and he related that one of his students had emailed him and invited him to graduation. He sacrificed the time and expense to travel because of one student, one more brilliant and this time, legendary answer.

Another teacher I had the good sense and fortune to hire quickly after the interview was Phyllis Fassio. Phyllis was a veteran elementary teacher that I convinced to transition into a key high school math position. Mrs. Fassio's classroom management skills were incredible. I became more organized as a principal by just walking into her class. Custodial staff loved her because they rarely had to clean the floors, boards or desks. She had a model classroom set up with her desk tucked into a corner and her students desks arranged so she could effortlessly walk up and down the aisles monitoring their progress and providing support. I envied her neat and easy to read handwriting. I am convinced that if I had Mrs. Fassio in elementary, my mom would have let me write with whatever hand I wanted, as long as it looked like Mrs. Fassio's. Not surprising, Mrs. Fassio was selected as a Top 10 Arizona teacher in 1994 by the Arizona Educational Foundation.

Mrs. Fassio taught with the same care and attention to detail. She broke problems down as far as she needed to until she saw that light go on in her students' eyes. Students crave teachers like Mrs. Fassio who blend highly organized classrooms with expert teaching and concern.

One such student was Sarah Baird. One day, Sarah was having a difficult day in Mrs. Fassio's class. This was not unusual and by Sarah's own admission, she had an attitude and academic grade problem at this time in her high school career. Mrs. Fassio calmly, yet firmly asked Sarah to step outside to have a conversation. According to Mrs. Fassio, she told Sarah she was better than her attitude and grades were showing. This was a turning point for Sarah and fast forward to 2009 – Sarah is being congratulated by Mrs. Fassio on stage at the Arizona Teacher of the Year Ceremony. Sarah Baird had just been named the Arizona Teacher of the Year. Sarah Baird, with Mrs. Fassio's guidance, had become an elementary math teacher, one legendary teacher inspiring another legendary teacher.

Legendary teachers develop, practice, and continually refine their classroom management skills. They understand the strong correlation between student learning and focused time on task. If you do the math, a typical school year is 186 days and a typical school day is seven hours; 186 days times 7 hours equals 1302 hours. A full year is 365 days and we are awake an average of 12 hours, 365 days times 12 hours equals 4,380 hours. 1302 divided by 4,380 is .297260 rounded and converted to percent is 30%. Mr. Serrell would be very proud.

If we know that students are in school with teachers only 30% of the year, distracted learning reduces this percentage to an alarming figure. Legendary teachers utilize effective classroom management to maximize every teaching moment and learning opportunity.

Legendary teachers have the courage to step up and step in when students need redirection and guidance and they never let their students get the red spot, even after graduation.

Chapter Nine

*Be Legendary. Know the symptoms of a stroke. Follow the American Heart Association's FAST guidelines:*

*Face drooping*
*Arm weakness*
*Speech Difficulty*
*Time to call 911 immediately*

*Chapter Nine*

# My Stroke of Luck

As much as I loved school, I admit that the first day back was difficult. I remember lying in bed eyes wide open, sun still shining, lamenting that summer was over. The sun was still up because we were shifting to school night savings time. School night bedtime was 7 p.m. and summer bedtime was whenever our batteries ran out on our flashlight as we played spot-em (night time hide and go seek) or looked for night crawlers. Bedtime at seven only could mean one thing. Tomorrow my teacher was going to asked me to write a paragraph about what I did this summer.

I didn't look forward to this assignment during my days as a student, not because I didn't have exciting summers but because I struggled with writing. One year I just stared at a blank sheet of paper as my 6th-grade teacher, Mrs. King, walked by and whispered, "Just write the title about the best part of your summer and the rest of the words will come easy."

In August 2011, as I sat at my desk, trying to write my faculty and staff welcome back to school address, I decided to take Mrs. King's advice, I typed the first words that popped into my head in bold letters centered on the top of the paper, "My Stroke of Luck."

On high school graduation day during the previous spring, I woke up early to get ready for an eighth grade recognition breakfast ceremony which was being held at the *University of Arizona*. When I got up, my body started to tell me something was not right. My balance was off and I was walking like a duck as I began my normal morning chores, watering the plants, feeding the dogs, retrieving the paper and showering. I was also not feeling well. My mind wasn't listening to my body and I proceeded to get dressed and drive to the ceremony.

As I drove, I was not feeling better and my parking in the parking structure seemed to be more challenging than normal. My body again was making the case that something was definitely wrong as I struggled to walk down the brick steps from where I parked on the third floor. My brain countered that I must be getting the start of a flu bug and that I should buck up and be strong. It was graduation day and I had not missed a graduation in 28 years. My brain had met its match. This time, I started slurring words when I greeted some teachers and students at the award ceremony. As I recall, I did not have much of an appetite and left soon after the awards. If parking the car was difficult, backing out and navigating my way down the winding parking structure was almost impossible. I did make it back to the office, and as hard as my body tried, it could not convince my stubborn brain that I should go to a doctor. I told the office staff I wasn't feeling good and I was going home to lie down. Against their advice, I said I would be back for graduation. When I arrived home, I threw up and got in bed. My brain thought it now had a good argument: "See, body, he threw up and that means he has a little bug." I woke not feeling better, got dressed, and didn't drive any better back to school as I found myself over steering the turns. I sat in my office in a funk and decided to wait as long as possible to put on that long, heavy, hot academic robe. I did try to answer some emails. I can't recall any flu affecting my ability to key board. I was a fast and accurate typist, maybe it was because of the right hand, left hand thing. On that day I was keyboarding at the usual speed but the words did not make any sense. I then stared at a pile of projects which needed grading for a graduate class I was teaching. I did make one good decision that day. I did not touch the projects.

I finally made my way out to the football field for graduation. When it was my turn to speak, I slurred and mumbled my way through my welcome and graduation address. I am sure parents and families figured I had gone to the bar before the ceremony. Not exactly the impression a superintendent wants to make, especially with a public budget vote on the horizon.

The next day, again against my family and my own body's wishes, I went to work. I needed to attend a year-end going away assembly for one of our principals. I could hardly walk on stage and I cried and hugged the principal three times. That was three times more than I had hugged him his entire career. My body finally won.

My first stroke of luck is that I finally listened to my family and co-workers who recognized I was demonstrating stroke symptoms. At their insistence, I called my physician and was directed to proceed immediately to the closest hospital emergency room.

My good fortune continued. The hospital stroke team quickly went into action, completing a number of triage tests and then rushed me in for an MRI. The tests confirmed that I had suffered a pons area stroke and I was admitted for observation and treatment. The pons area is part of the brain stem that contains bundles of nerves carrying movement and sensory messages between the brain and body. A small stroke in this area can have significant consequences because of the concentration of electrical circuits, which lose blood supply as a result of a clot or hemorrhage.

Again, I was lucky to have my family and an entire medical team devoted to helping my obstinate brain understand I had two choices — I could be a stroke victim or a stroke patient. After a great deal of resistance and denial, I chose patient, a critical decision for recovery. Being a stroke patient means you commit to a recovery plan, which means staying away from work, along with undertaking rigorous physical and speech therapy.

Relearning is humbling and frustrating. I was lucky to have great therapists, who helped me work on balance and eye-hand coordination, along with regaining my speech and cognitive reasoning skills. I first approached therapy as something my family and friends wanted and needed more than me. Reflecting, my speech therapist should have put me in permanent time out. During our first session, I fought her all the way until she gave me a test that I thought I would have no problem with, naming words that start with random letters of the alphabet. H, K, M, and even N, my mind was blank and I could not think of or say one word.

I now started to experience a combination of panic, sadness, and frustration. The realization finally set in, I needed therapy. After making additional appointments for the rest of the month, I cried on my way home. When I arrived at home, Self-1 and Self-2 started arguing: Self-2 – "What if I don't fully recover? Looks like you might miss your first graduation next year." Self-1 – "Buck up buddy, you just need to work hard; you can do this." Again, I was lucky because Self-1 won the debate. I became determined to follow my doctors, family, and therapists orders and work diligently at recovery.

Like the advice every legendary teacher in my life gave me, recovery got harder before it got easier. On the second visit, my speech therapist had me do a cognitive puzzle she called wedding cake which involved moving different sized round wooden discs from one pole to another pole. The task required that you make the moves without having a larger disc on top of a smaller disc. It looked easy and I was anxious to prove that maybe I could cancel a few of my appointments. I jumped at the chance and started fast and then hit a wall, gave up and cried. I went home, found a virtual version on line and spend the entire weekend learning the moves by rote. I couldn't wait to return to therapy on Tuesday. At the end of therapy, my therapist went to her storage cabinet and pulled out the wedding cake puzzle. I was doing a mental fist pump even before she placed it in front of me. Right before she set it down, she mentioned, "Let's try five discs instead of four." She caught me, I had practiced with only four. This is one example of how my therapist knew that the only way to get better is to keep being challenged. The physical therapists followed suit with exercises which seemed to get more painful every week and tears would also flow.

I thought I knew everything about legendary teaching and learning. Luckily, my stroke helped me discover I still have more to learn. Now, each time I walk into a classroom, I have a new appreciation for how important it is for the teacher to be patient and caring while teaching students a new skill. This stroke also made me aware of the power of the teacher's approval when students make even small progress toward a goal. As important, my stroke gave me a deeper perspective and understanding of the fine line between frustration being a motivator for learning and frustration making students shut down. Legendary teachers create wedding cake like puzzles every day, adding discs when students get comfortable, while providing a safe and supporting place to practice trial and error and allow crying every now and then.

I was really lucky that summer because I had a reason and the time to learn as much as I could about strokes. Causes of stroke, prevention of stroke, stroke treatment, brain anatomy and chemistry dominated my search engine. I had an insatiable need to read any books and research I could get my hands on. I viewed videos showing blood flow to the brain and what occurs when blood flow is stopped by a clot or a bleed. I had my speech therapist demonstrate on a visual mannequin the swallow muscles that were affected and explain why my speech slurred. I requested and studied the hospital MRI pictures of my brain.

A stroke is serious and according to the *American Heart and Stroke Association*, the third largest cause of death in the United States. Therefore, I want to be careful with my next legendary teacher lesson. When I use my stroke as a metaphor to legendary teachers who possess that special skill to trigger a student's curiosity and motivate them to learn, I am trying to communicate an 'aha' moment that I had as a result of the stroke and not in any way diminish the importance of preventing and treating strokes. This might qualify as one of my most important back-to-school essays and legendary teacher stories if it promotes awareness of stroke and can help save lives.

We all need to know the stroke risk factors, which include some you can control, such as tobacco smoke, obesity, diabetes, physical inactivity, high cholesterol and high blood pressure, and some you can't, such as family history and increasing age. We need to recognize the early warning signs, which according to the *American Heart and Stroke Association* include a drooping face, arm numbness and speech difficulty. We need to understand the importance of calling 911 and getting medical help as soon as possible and not wait like I did.

My personal legendary teacher lesson was that you can do something about the factors you can control and make some changes in your life. Don't sweat the small stuff, and be sure to hug your family and friends more than three times a day. I wonder how Mrs. King would assess this essay. I hope it deserves an A, because I can't handle a B. Just ask my speech therapist.

*Chapter Ten*

*Legendary teachers*
*most likely had*
*legendary teachers.*

# The Legendary Teacher Code

Dad was finishing up cleaning his law office and I was helping with the last task, packing up his law books. My dad was retiring after practicing law in the same town in the same place for over forty years. The original shingle with his name, William Clement, Attorney at Law, was still hanging outside his office in the home he grew up in. Early in his career, my dad made a choice to work in the town he grew up in and sacrifice the big salary and perks that came with a larger law firm. He made that choice for many reasons; his family and his community were top of the list. If you talked to his clients and asked them to describe my dad in one word, they would without hesitation reply "honest."

My dad rarely charged the recommended fees for his services and would often take goods and services in trade for his legal advice when a client could not pay. One winter day, I was driving to school and hit an icy patch causing the station wagon to take out a mail box. I know by now you are concerned. I am scheduled to renew my driver's license in 2018. If it makes you feel more at ease, feel free to contact the Arizona Motor Vehicle Division and request I take a road test. When I told my dad about my accident, he asked me where the house was. I described the house and told him it was at the corner of Mill Lake Road and M-40. He then named the person living there and said we are now even. The mail box owner had owed my dad for legal services and had not paid for over two years. I am sure the value of the old mail box did not equal the owed fees, but that was how my dad lived his life and his law practice.

Although I did not take out the mail box on purpose, I was secretly hoping that the damage was going to be enough to motivate my parents to buy a newer more hip car. Growing up, we always had a station wagon. In 1966, we took our big cross country trip driving from Gobles to Denver in a station wagon with the back seat that faced the opposite direction. I don't know which car designer in Detroit thought of this idea but it is obvious that they never suffered from motion sickness like me. Logic would call for the kid with the worst case to be able to sit facing forward. Birth order and seniority trumped logic on this trip. We had many side trips planned as we traveled through the Badlands and many unplanned rest area stops. Until he passed away, my dad always had a station wagon. When my parents were traveling, one of his favorites broke down outside Atlanta. He wrote and sent all the kids an obituary for the car along with a picture of the new car he purchased, same make, model and color.

As we were loading the books in the station wagon getting ready to deliver them to the new lawyer in town who had purchased them, I recall discussing the recent changes in the legal field, particularly the fact that lawyers were beginning to advertise. That bothered my dad and he talked about the fact that he believed that advertising violated the code of ethics he signed when he received his degree and was admitted to the *American Bar Association*.

Like many memories, there was a reason this discussion has stayed fresh in my mind for over twenty years. Although formally, he signed the code after he passed his Bar exam, in reality, he signed the code early in life, with his parents guiding his hand, then his signature became stronger and bolder as he progressed through elementary, high school, undergraduate and law school.

The legendary teachers spotlighted in this book all followed an unwritten code of ethics which also was influenced by their parents and legendary teachers along with hours of professional training and practice. Their shared values, beliefs, commitment and expert skills inspired me to develop the Legendary Teacher Code.

Legendary teachers strive to help students discover and understand concepts. Legendary teachers do not easily give up the answer; rather they create different levels of puzzles and mazes which promote inquiry. Discovery by definition requires exploration, hitting dead ends, failure, trial and error, patience, and time. Legendary teachers understand that if their instructional lesson is designed to promote student experimentation, their students will create new knowledge which will be deep, transferable and retained. Mr. Serrell could have stood in front of his seventh grade class and lectured about probability and written some equations along with flipping a coin a couple of times. It would have taken less time and caused less hassle. He could have handed out ditto sheets after his lecture and settled into his teacher desk, graded papers and occasionally told us to get to work until the bell rang. Students don't talk about those teachers at their reunions.

Legendary teachers engage students in creative learning activities. Neurologists often explain the learning process as brain neurons firing and then wiring together. Without the fire, no wire. Without a teacher engaging students, no fire. Legendary teachers plan activities which focus on overt and covert active participation and they constantly adjust their plan when they sense students are getting the red spot. They know the right time to pose that thought provoking question that puts everyone on notice, starting the firing process, waits for the wire, and then randomly calls on someone for not only the answer, but follows up with more questions to get at the why. Think about how the worm moves and I am going to call on someone to give their hypothesis. Explain your hypothesis and write it down in your lab dissection notes. Nic, what was the name of the blood vessel you just sliced into? I will get you another specimen for your tray. I was probably using my left hand. Mr. Davis was a brain neuron pyromaniac.

Legendary teachers connect learning to the past, present, and future. After my parents passed away, my brothers got together and decided we were going to have to clean out the garage. It was a large two car standalone garage which never saw the family station wagon or any other car. We rented a big roll off dumpster and started early in the morning to clean and toss the junk that had accumulated over the years. At lunch, the garage was totally clean and empty and the roll off was clean and empty. People seeing all our stuff spread out on the driveway started to drive in thinking we were having a garage sale. That irritated us because every item had some connection to one of us which kept it out of the dumpster. We agreed we had to let go and decided we would start throwing fast and not have everyone touch every item. It was going well until I picked up this old small piece of curved metal. It was red and for some reason, I stopped and cleaned off some writing on one side and made out the word Spitfire. Instantly I knew what it was, the chain guard from my Spitfire bike. I stood in a daze as memories associated with that bike filled my brain. Christmas Day when I found it was under the tree; riding to Grandma's house; wiping out in a gravel parking lot next to school; and riding to buy ice cream from Dennis Hurlbut's new soft serve ice cream truck. I threw it over the dumpster and faked liked I needed a bathroom break, picked up my chain guard, and hid it in my suitcase for a safe trip back to be displayed in my office. Legendary teachers transform content to create the same powerful connection. Mr. Potts answered that annoying question, why do I have to learn this and when am I ever going to need it, before I had a chance to ask.

Legendary teachers adapt their methods and assessment to meet diverse learning styles. If you asked my mother, she would have told you that I was not a very good listener. She could tell me something over and over, which she often did, but if she showed me how to do something, I picked it up much quicker. Legendary teachers have developed incredible intuition when assessing student learning styles. They read students eyes, their body language, their voice intonation, and adapt their teaching so the light bulb goes on. Trial and error is a critical part of the teaching process. Legendary teachers constantly ask and answer the question, "Did I astound my students today?" If they are not satisfied with the answer, legendary teachers change their methods.

Legendary teachers create and maintain dynamic learning environments. What is a dynamic learning environment? Legendary teachers know that only students can answer that question. The student focus group described the perfect teacher as inspiring, balanced, creative, and has a class pet. Legendary teachers understand that student perception is their reality and you have to ask the right questions and actively listen. Mr. Fitzpatrick would have changed the wording to this part of the code to: Legendary teachers create a no red spot zone.

Legendary teachers continue to improve their content knowledge base and their teaching skills. As mentioned in previous stories, I grew up in a three story house. When I

was very young, I would often get lost at night going back
to my room after going to the bathroom. I either couldn't
find the lights or wasn't tall enough to reach the switch. My
parents complicated my internal GPS system by continually
renovating and adding new rooms to the maze. During the
Cuban Missile Crisis, they built a bomb shelter which if you
ended up down there, you might not be found for days or
until my mom went down to raid the food closet. As I got
older, I started to really learn the house layout and could sneak
around at night even navigating my way to the bomb shelter
for some crackers and peanut butter. I developed deep content
knowledge of my house. After lots of practice, trial and error,
and a few tears while curled up in a ball on the bathroom floor,
I created a 3-D picture in my brain. Legendary teachers do the
same with content and pedagogy. They constantly are going
through professional development to sharpen their 3-D image.
Legendary teachers are able to take that image and transform
it enabling their students to navigate complex and complicated
subject matter houses.

My dad had few things hanging on his wall. One was a
picture of Abe Lincoln. Another was his law school diploma
from the *University of Michigan*. I also remember seeing his code
of ethics framed and located where every client could see. If
given the opportunity, Mr. Serrell, Mr. Potts, Mrs. King, Miss
Ringle, Mr. Davis, Miss Filley, Mrs. Fassio, Mr. Fitzpatrick, and
Mr. Wade would have framed and pasted this code on a shingle
outside their classroom door.

*Legendary Teachers...*

- Strive to help students discover and understand concepts.

- Engage students in creative learning activities.

- Connect learning to the past, present and future.

- Adapt their methods and assessments to meet diverse learning styles.

- Create and maintain dynamic learning environments.

- Continue to improve their content knowledge base and teaching skills.

# *Epilogue*

This book represents a major step towards fulfilling my dream to honor and celebrate all teachers for the incredible influence they have on the lives of their students.

This is a great feeling yet I still have that nagging anxiety like I did when I thought I finished helping a neighbor spring clean her kitchen. Our neighbor, Mrs. Feeley, had reached the age when she couldn't get all the pots and pans out of her cabinets. I was young and small enough to crawl through like a ferret and get them out so they could be cleaned. Although there were still cabinets with pots hidden in those dark corners, I came home after lunch. I am sure Mrs. Feeley felt guilty about keeping me away from playing on a beautiful summer day. My mom greeted me at the door and immediately sent me back to help finish the job.

I have enough issues and regrets with red boots, football, and falling on the water ski ramp, that I cannot deal with not doing something to "finish" my dream.

Legendary teachers need support while they are still mortal. I want to try and do my part by starting a foundation where teachers can apply to receive small grants to fund classroom projects, activities and field trips which they often fund from their own pockets. This foundation called the "Teachers Change Brains Micro Grant Fund" will be supported through the profits from the sale of this book and other donations. Teachers interested in applying for a grant can go to *www.legendaryteacher.com* for more information and access to an on-line grant application.

Help me convince my mom that I can come back in the house, apply for a grant and buy another copy of this book for a friend.

I welcome any comments, feedback and questions regarding this book. Please contact me at *Nicholas.clement@nau.edu.*